Money Management

Easy as 1, 2, 3

Money Management: Easy as 1, 2, 3
by Ernest Burley, Jr.
Foreword by Michelle Singletary

Published by V.I.T.A.L. Visions Publishing, Inc.
13621 Annapolis Rd., Bowie, MD 20720
301-262-2600

This book is available in volume for qualifying organizations.

This material is intended for informational purposes only. This material is not meant to
replace the advice of legal, financial, or other professional counsel. Individuals should always
gather and consider more than one source of information in order to make well-informed
decisions. Ernest Burley, Jr. and the publisher make no guarantee of results from the use of
this material and are not responsible for any misuse of this material.

Cover design by Shalon Simpson
Interior design & layout by Pneuma Books. Visit : www.pneumabooks.com

Publisher's Cataloging-In-Publication Data
(Prepared by The Donohue Group, Inc.)

Burley, Ernest.

Money management : easy as 1, 2, 3 / by Ernest Burley, Jr. ; and a foreword by
Michelle Singletary.

p. ; cm.

ISBN: 978-0-615-31524-9

1. Finance, Personal--Popular works. 2. Finance--Popular works. I. Singletary,
Michelle. II. Title.

HG179 .B87 2009
332.024   2009936566

PRINTED IN THE UNITED STATES OF AMERICA

15 14 13 12 11 10 09   01 02 03 04 05 06 07

Money
Management
Easy as 1, 2, 3

by Ernest Burley, Jr.,

CFP®, ChFC®, CPCU®, AIS

and a Foreword by Michelle Singletary,
personal finance columnist, *The Washington Post*

V.I.T.A.L. VISIONS PUBLISHING, INC.
Bowie, MD

Easy as 1 2 3

Contents

Easy as 1 2 3

Foreword

The first time I met Ernest, he was ushering me to my seat at our church. He wasn't just being nice; he was an usher, serving on Sundays. At the time I had no idea that behind his infectious smile was a man with a strong passion to teach people how to handle their money.

Once I made that discovery, I grabbed Ernest to take part in a financial ministry I direct at First Baptist Church of Glenarden. The ministry, Prosperity Partners, matches people who are good stewards over their money (Senior Partners) with individuals who have financial challenges (Junior Partners). Ernest is a Senior Partner helping to mentor couples and men on better money management techniques.

I'm telling you all of this because it shows the character of the man who in this book is trying to help you better manage your money. He didn't have to sign up to volunteer his time in this labor-intensive ministry, but he did. This information is important for you to know because no matter what book you read or financial adviser you hire, you need to know that person has your interests at heart first. There is a lot of bad financial advice out there, and you need to look at the person giving you information about your money.

Money Management: Easy as 1, 2, 3 lives up to its title. It's an accessible easy read with good basic advice in three simple chapters. And don't mistake short and simple for unsophisticated. In fact, that's the problem many people have when it comes to their finances. They think the more complicated something sounds the more money they will make. It's that belief that causes so many investors to be duped into bogus investment schemes.

I love that this book starts where all good money management should begin—with the "b" word. Yes, that's b for a budget. The road to richness as Ernest lays out starts with getting control of the money coming in and going out. That's the first step.

The second step, as you will read, is finding the right place for your money. And the last easy road to good stewardship is protecting your assets and lifestyle with the right money decisions.

It won't take you long to go through this book and yet the practical and sage financial advice will last you a lifetime.

~Michelle Singletary
Nationally Syndicated Personal Finance Columnist
The Washington Post

Easy as 1 2 3

Easy as 1 2 3

Preface

I wrote this book because I know people want to do better with their money. They want to make good decisions for themselves and their families. The trouble is that many people weren't given a proper example to follow as they grew up, so they repeat the mistakes they saw. Other people weren't given any example or they simply didn't notice one, so they're winging it with their finances. Whatever the reason, it's not productive to continue mismanaging your money. The good news is that there's no reason to stay stuck in the rut of financial depression and bondage.

Money management may seem simple and basic to some, but to others it is a difficult thing to do. Those who find it difficult often feel paralyzed. They may not know whom to turn to for good financial advice. They may not have the money to pay for financial advice. They may be turned off by money topics. They may have received bad advice in the past and feel paranoid as a result. They may find financial terminology confusing so the topic of money is scary to them. Or, they may simply feel overwhelmed by all they don't know.

I have worked with people who have experienced all these fears and concerns, and I have seen their financial lives turn around. When people begin to learn how to properly manage their money, they get pretty excited. It's like a light bulb has been turned on. They get a glimmer of hope.

I'm here to make money management clear, simple, and easy to understand. I want to help you see how useful basic money management techniques can be. I'm here to demystify things that you may find confusing and shine the light on some things you may have overlooked. I'm here to encourage you. You can do it. Baby steps are all you need to get started. I'm here to get you started down the road to proper money management!

Let me tell you a little about myself. I am a CERTIFIED FINANCIAL PLANNER™ practitioner and a Chartered Financial Consultant® who has over twenty years of experience helping people in the insurance and financial services arena. I also hold the CPCU® designation (Chartered Property Casualty Underwriter) and AIS designation (Associate in Insurance Services). The certifications are great, but the hands-on experience allows me to speak from a point of knowledge and facts. I'm not offering you hypothetical situations or unjustifiable conclusions or speaking from what I have heard, read, or merely researched. I'm speaking from experience in the trenches in various capacities.

I started my career handling property damage and liability claims for a major insurance company. This experience gave me a deep-rooted knowledge of claim handling procedures, insurance policies, and insurance coverage along with their practical application. I also gathered an array of knowledge on excluded coverages and inadequate coverage. When you've paid millions of dollars on a multitude of claims, you find out what type of protection people really need and how they are affected when they have a gap in their protection. You also see how well people continue their lives when they are properly protected.

Eventually, I opened my own insurance and financial services firm. I offer various insurance and financial products to meet clients' needs. I started working toward obtaining various designations early in my career and continued through my years as the owner of Burley Insurance and Financial Services, Inc^{SM}. During my career as a financial services professional, I've been invited to give dozens of presentations to various groups. The presentations have ranged from financial services/products to insurance to entrepreneurship to financial planning and more.

I've been blessed to run a successful practice. I've received many awards, plaques, and reward trips due to the production that has flowed from my office. This is all due to the rapport I build with my clients and others in the community based on trust, integrity, and compassion. I look out for clients' best interests and offer them the products and services they need.

As a CERTIFIED FINANCIAL PLANNER™ practitioner and Chartered Financial Consultant®, I meet with clients to discuss their goals, their dreams, their budgets, their concerns — their everything. Some of my clients won't even do anything with their money until they speak with me. My experiences helping, meeting, and speaking with people has inspired me to write this book. I am also currently mentoring a fellow financial services professional. His inquiries and goals also have a place in this book.

My concern for clients and their finances stems from a deep-seated passion to help people achieve and succeed. By following some basic principles, I know people can turn around their money situations and get back on track. Or, they can get on track in the first place. I've spoken to so many people who have fallen victim to schemes and lost thousands of dollars—and in some cases even hundreds of thousands of dollars—because they didn't follow the basic principles I'm going to discuss in this book. This book is for them. This book is for you.

~Ernest Burley, Jr.

Easy as 1 2 3

Easy as 1 2 3

Easy as 1, 2, 3

This book is designed to give you easy steps to financial success. These steps are not complicated, so this book is easy to read. The basic concepts in this book should put you on the right path with your money. These concepts apply whether you have no money, a little money, or a lot of money. Implementing the tools in this book will enable you to properly manage your money and escape the feeling of drowning that so many people have about their finances. You *can* escape the frustrating pit of financial bondage; and in reading this book, you are taking the first step to do just that. Better still, once you help yourself, you can help others. You can be an example for others to follow—your family, friends, and even your children. The snowball effect is powerful, so let's get rolling!

Many people find it difficult to meet their everyday financial needs and live in peace. As responsibilities grow, it gets more and more difficult to manage. Some people never seem to see the light at the end of the tunnel. They just know they're in a tunnel. My goal is to show you the light and deliver you into the light at the end of the tunnel so you can live there and stay there, in peace.

The biggest reason people have financial problems is mismanagement of their money. If you develop *and implement* the basic principles, you *will* properly handle your money and you will move up the chain of financial success. You don't always have to hover around the bottom. A simple plan of action will set everything in motion.

When people hear the words *financial planning*, they think a lot of different things. Here are some thoughts people commonly have when they consider the idea of financial planning:

- It's too complicated.

- That's for rich people.

- You need money to have a financial plan.

- Financial planning is all about sacrifice.

- It's not for me.

- I'm not ready for that yet.

- I don't have time to do that.

- I can manage.

- I'll get around to it next year.

- I'll ask around and see what my friends and colleagues are doing.

There are a million reasons not to plan, but none of those reasons helps you. I deliberately made this book short, to-the-point, and easy to understand because I wanted to eliminate the possibility of making excuses. There are no pages filled with confusing terminology or formulas you can't remember or use. I want to deflate the air of complication in the financial planning process and give you solid, simple, and basic principles to live by. In short, I'm trying to say now *there is no excuse!*

You don't have to be rich to have a financial plan. As a matter of fact, the less money you have, the more imperative it is to have a financial plan. Why? Because you have less room for error. A $100, $1,000, or $5,000 (or more) error in judgment will have a more adverse affect on a person earning $50,000 a year than on a person earning $500,000 a year.

If you follow the basic principles in this book, you will be well on your way to financial success. This doesn't necessarily mean you'll become rich. You very well may climb the ladder to riches and wealth, but this book is designed to give you the tools you need to handle what you have now and properly manage it so you can move to the next level—and the next level and the next level. Financial success involves properly managing the funds you have and living a life you can afford coupled with a life you desire.

Easy as 1 2 3

Chapter One

Cash Flow
and Budgeting

O ne of the questions I frequently hear as I help people with their finances is the most basic and important one of all: "How am I going to make it with my limited income and seemingly unlimited bills?" If you feel that way, you are not alone. It's a very common question. That brings us to the starting block of financial planning. The first process everyone should go through in developing a financial plan is a cash flow analysis. Then you should move immediately into establishing a budget. Now, I remember that I promised no fancy terminology. A cash flow analysis is just the proper term for looking at "**Money In** versus **Money Out**." Let's call it M.I.M.O., which is short for Money In Money Out.

Looking at your M.I.M.O. may be the most difficult step in this whole process. Please hear me on this. I understand the emotional stress and pain it may take to actually write down how you've been spending your money. I know it will take a lot of courage to do it. I'm applauding you already, and I want to assure you that you will love the fact you did it (sooner than you can imagine). Congratulate yourself for taking the first step to getting your finances in order. This may be the most important step in your financial life. Take pride in the fact that you have made a conscientious decision to improve your financial picture.

M.I.M.O. is short for Money In Money Out.

If there are two people going through this process (that is, if you're doing this with your spouse or significant other), I'm going to ask both parties to be sensitive to each other. Go into this section with a positive attitude and a mutual agreement that neither of you will pass judgment on the other—no matter how much you may want to. Keep an open heart and be compassionate. None of us is perfect. Let's help each other through the process. Before you say something to the other person, think about it. Also, proactively speak with good intentions. Watch the tone and content of your comments. Say to yourself, "How will this statement be interpreted?" Ask yourself, "How can I soften my comment or tone? How can I speak in a mild and optimistic manner?" Or, "How would I like this comment if it were directed at me?"

Here's another tip. Watch your facial expressions and body language. My wife likes to interpret my body language. She knows if my forehead is wrinkled while we're communicating that there may be some concern. She also knows my eyes tell a lot about what I'm thinking. You know yourself. So, before starting this exercise please control these three elements — voice/comments, body language, and facial expressions. That means no sighing, grunting, folding arms, glaring stares, deafening silence, rolling eyes, demeaning comments, sharp or sarcastic tones, flailing of arms, pouting, complaining, and so forth. Let's only use the past actions as a benchmark of where not to return. Look forward from today. Compliment and support each other for having the mindset to straighten out your finances from this point forward.

Easy as 1 2 3

If you're doing this with your spouse or significant other, I'm going to ask both parties to be sensitive to each other.

This is a team effort and a team-building exercise. Do not condemn one another but build up each other. Use this exercise constructively to strengthen your relationship and strengthen your family's financial health. There are three prominent reasons for marital problems — communication, sex, and MONEY. I can't help you with the first two. Those aren't my areas of expertise, but I think I have a good word for you on the topic of money. Just think: you can improve your financial situation and your marriage!

If you are going through the process by yourself, it should be somewhat easier since you won't have another person to consider. Be honest and real with yourself though. Lay it out there. The only way to make a positive change is to fully disclose the facts and possess a genuine desire to change. If you're doing this alone, I suggest you partner with someone who can hold you accountable. This should be someone who makes wise decisions with their money. Someone who will tell you the truth and encourage you to do the right thing rather than pacify you or justify your errant actions.

Here are the steps we'll go through in this chapter. Complete these steps and you will be taking a giant leap forward in money management:

- **Step 1**: Complete the cash flow analysis (M.I.M.O.) worksheet. You will want to input accurate information because garbage in equals garbage out. Your checkbook, bank account statement and credit card statement should give you the figures you need to complete the cash flow analysis.

Easy as 1 2 3

If you're single and going through this process alone, I suggest you partner with someone who can hold you accountable.

- **Step 2**: Review M.I.M.O. in detail. Be honest. Look at each category and expense. Decide whether each expense is a "want" or a "need." Get rid of as many "wants" as possible so you can meet your actual "needs."

- **Step 3**: Make adjustments based on this review. Eliminate obvious waste areas and look for ways any expenses can be reduced. Make the hard decisions. Sacrifice some things in the short term to reap long-term rewards. You may have to get very strict for several months or even a year or two, but the results will be worth it. You didn't mess up your finances in one or two months so it's going to take more than one or two months to correct them. Look towards the horizon though. After your intense crunch time, you'll enjoy decades of financial bliss!

- **Step 4**: Use extra funds (from eliminated or reduced spending) to pay down debt and/or obtain products that are beneficial to your family and finances (emergency savings, disability protection, IRA, and so forth).

Your M.I.M.O.

There's no avoiding it. It's time to take a deep look at your cash flow. You will do this by filling out the budget calculator I've provided in worksheet 1. You'll fill in your income and expenses using the actual numbers of what comes in (income) and what goes out (expenses). Make sure your numbers are accurate.

Easy as 1 2 3

Gather your checkbook, credit card statement(s), and bank statement so you can accurately complete the worksheet.

Worksheet 1 is a general, easy-to-follow worksheet that includes the major categories any budget calculator should have. There are numerous budget calculators available online and in books. If there's one you prefer to use, please feel free to use that one. Be sure to leave room for miscellaneous expenses, because everyone's situation is different. However, most of your expenses should fall into one of the categories we'll review.

Gather your checkbook, credit card statement(s), and bank statement so you can accurately complete the worksheet. You want to be thorough and catch ALL your expenses on this worksheet. You need to account for every penny spent so you can move forward with correct information, and the documents I mentioned should track all of your money movement.

An important side note. If you don't have a bank account, please open one. Dealing in money orders and cash only is not a good way to handle your finances. What if you lose your money order(s) or misplace the cash? What if someone steals the money orders or cash? That money is gone. If you have a checking account, you can order new checks, place a stop payment on a stolen check, and even be reimbursed for fraudulent activity on your account. Handle your bills and finances with a checking account.

Here's your budget calculator. Time to get to work. Please fill out your *monthly* expenses in each category of Worksheet 1 over the next few pages.

Easy as 1 2 3

Worksheet 1: Cash Flow Analysis: Money In Money Out

Expense	Monthly Cost
Home Expenses	
Mortgage or rent	
Property taxes	
Home or renters insurance	
HOA/COA (Home/Condo Assn. Fee)	
Community dues	
Alarm monitoring	
Gas	
Electric	
Home phone	
Cell phone	
Cable	
Water	
Internet	
Service contracts (hvac, appliances…)	
Repairs/upgrades	
Miscellaneous (be specific)	
Total Monthly Home Expenses	
Food Expenses	
Groceries	
Lunch (parents and children)	
Eating out (during the week)	
Eating out (on weekends)	
Snacks (throughout the day)	
Total Monthly Food Expenses	
(Table continued on the next page)	

Loan Payments	
Auto loan(s)	
2nd and/or 3rd mortgage	
Line of credit	
Student loan(s)	
*Credit card(s)	
Consolidated loan(s)	
Other debt payments	
Total Monthly Loan Expenses	
Transportation Expenses	
Fuel	
Service/maintenance on vehicle	
Public transportation	
Parking	
Repairs	
Total Monthly Transportation Expenses	
Saving/Investing	
Savings	
Retirement plan at work	
IRA(s)	
Mutual Fund(s)	
Annuity(ies)	
Education savings	
Stock purchases	
Total Monthly Savings Expenses	
Healthcare Expenses	
Co-payments	
Regular prescriptions	
Regular therapy (physical or mental)	
Total Monthly Health Care Expenses	
(Table continued on the next page)	

Insurance Payments	
Health	
Life	
Disability	
Long-term care	
Auto	
Business	
Other	
Total Monthly Insurance Expenses	
Clothing	
Adult clothing	
Children's clothing	
Children's school uniforms	
Total Monthly Clothing Expenses	
Miscellaneous (men and women)	
Vacation(s)/Family Travel	
Special occasions	
Tuition	
Child care	
Before care	
After care	
Alimony	
Child support	
Children's summer activities (camp, etc.)	
Children's extracurricular activities (sports, lessons, etc.)	
Charitable contributions	
Hair	
Manicure	
Pedicure	
Entertainment (movies, sporting events, etc.)	
(Table continued on the next page)	

Recreation (bowling, golf, etc.)	
Pet care	
Drycleaners	
Postage	
Store memberships (BJ's, Costco, etc.)	
Gym membership	
Publications (magazines, etc.)	
Other	
Total Monthly Miscellaneous Expenses	
Income	
Salary	
Bonuses	
Pension	
Annuity	
Alimony	
Child support	
Interest from investments	
Rental income	
Total Income	
Taxes	
Federal income taxes	
State income taxes	
FICA withholding	
Medicare withholding	
Local and property taxes	
Total Monthly Taxes	
Credit card amounts due can fluctuate.	

Understanding Your Worksheet

As you completed the worksheet, you filled out your monthly expenses as well as your income. Use the worksheet to calculate your net income (income minus taxes, which is also known as adjusted gross income or AGI.) For an example, let's suppose your total annual income is $50,000 and your taxes are $12,500 (25 percent tax bracket). In that case, you will be left with approximately $37,500 to work with. (Please note that in the United States, we have a progressive tax system, not a flat tax. Different income levels pay different tax rates.) Next you should subtract your expenses from your adjusted gross income. If your expenses total $2,500 a month, that equals $30,000 a year.

In this scenario there is a cash "surplus" of $7,500 ($37,500 - $30,000). That's good! You want to have surplus. On the other hand, if your monthly expenses are $3,200 a month, that equals $38,400 a year and you have a cash "deficit" of $900 a year ($37,500 - $38,400). That's not good.

Once you've completed the cash flow analysis worksheet and you have your final number, we can move to the review stage. Your final number will either be a positive cash flow figure (more money coming in than going out; a surplus) or a negative cash flow figure (more money going out than coming in; a deficit). I haven't ever seen anyone hit a perfect 0 (M.I. = M.O.).

Regardless of whether the figure is positive or negative, the review process is the next step. The same principles apply to those with plenty and those with little: decrease expenses where you can, and increase income if you can. Decrease expenses by following the budget *and* trimming some extras. Increase income by obtaining a second job, going for a promotion, or changing jobs.

Reviewing Your Results

Easy as 1 2 3

Review each expense in the worksheet to determine whether you can reduce or eliminate that expense. You may find that some expenses can be eliminated entirely. For instance, do you rarely use your home phone and tend to rely entirely on your cell phone? Could you eliminate your home phone? Or perhaps you eat out for lunch during the workweek. Can you consider eliminating that expense? Some expenses can't be eliminated, but they can be reduced. You may be able to reduce expenses by shopping around for new car insurance or you may be able to reduce your cable bill by cutting out the premium channels. If you have a cash deficit (your M.O. exceeds your M.I.), you will have some work to do and some decisions to make.

Cut back first on the things that have the least benefit. Prioritize the bills that will cause the greatest negative repercussions if not paid.

People get caught up in what they think they need, and they often confuse wants with needs. You don't need cable or the new upgraded cell phone. You don't need a new outfit or that plasma TV. Our culture is confused about the definition of *need*. Many people will justify their wants based on habit (what they've gotten used to or accustomed to) or flat out greed. To these folks, discussing "needs" instead of "wants" is like going to a barren, desolate island. It's unthinkable! Sometimes they get sensitive about it too. People have said to me with outrage, "You mean you want me to give up cable?" Ah, yes, I do—because it will save you $100 a month!

Here's another way to look at it. If your finances are tight and you have to make some cutbacks, look at the things that have the least benefit to cut back on first. Prioritize the bills that will cause the greatest negative repercussions if not paid. Let's do a quick exercise to demonstrate. Which bill can have a greater negative repercussion if not paid, cell phone or health insurance? Hmm. What's the worse that can happen if you don't pay the cell phone? They cut it off (temporarily or permanently). What's the worse thing that can happen if you don't pay that health insurance bill? Someone could get sick or injured and you could go bankrupt trying to pay the medical bills. These answers are easy if you are real with yourself. Do the right thing.

If you're in financial trouble (your M.O. exceeds your M.I.) why would you continue your same actions? That's like drowning but not removing the heavy weights on your ankles. You're constantly going under the water but you won't let go of the weights that are pulling you under. What sense does that make? Well, your old way of thinking may be weighing you down. Realign your thinking to the correct definition of a need. Check through your cash flow analysis for wants disguised as needs and eliminate them if necessary.

You will have to make sure there is no waste in your cash flow. One important area to review is your "cash" usage, which brings us to the important topic of ATM withdrawals. ATM withdrawals account for a lot of miscellaneous wasted cash that's hard to track. I don't recommend the use of ATM withdrawals except in rare instances when you need a small amount of pocket money for cash situations. For instance, some parking lots only take cash for special-event parking. An ATM withdrawal should be avoided whenever possible. Use your debit card instead. This will allow you to keep track of those expenses.

> Easy as 1 2 3
>
> If you're in financial trouble (your M.O. exceeds your M.I.) why would you continue your same actions? That's like drowning but not removing the heavy weights on your ankles.

Most businesses accept a Visa® debit card. If the business is "cash only," make sure you withdraw the exact amount needed for that transaction. When you do need to access an ATM, please use your own bank's ATM. Why pay someone else a fee to get your money? That is a waste! Exhaust all efforts to use your own bank's ATM. If you can't find one, you can buy something you need (or will need soon enough) at the store and get cash back from your debit card for free. You need to be wise with your money. ATM withdrawals and bank ATM fees account for a lot of "mystery money." Mystery money is the money you can't find. You had it, but — poof — now it's gone.

ATM withdrawals account for a lot of miscellaneous wasted cash that's hard to track. I don't recommend the use of ATM withdrawals.

Probably one of the simplest ways to reduce your expenses is to stop eating out. When I get together with clients to review their finances, I often see hundreds of dollars a month spent each month eating out. Yet, these same people are crying that they're broke. Let me give you an example from a presentation I gave on money management and budgeting. I asked a person in the audience to give me the rundown on her daily eating out. Here's what she reported:

- Each weekday morning she goes to Starbucks and spends $7.

- Each weekday for lunch she eats out, which costs her an average of $10.

- She buys sodas and snacks throughout the day, which amount to about $5.

- She doesn't cook, so she eats out almost every night, which costs her another $10-plus.

One of the simplest ways to reduce your expenses is to stop eating out.

Using these figures, the total adds up to $32 per day. Multiply that number by five for the five-day workweek and the total is $160. Then we need to multiply that number by the four weeks in a month and we get the total of $640 per month! Stunning, isn't it? Wait, that's not all. This figure is just during the workweek. How about weekends? Well, of course she goes out with friends over the weekend and spends another $30-$40 minimum at restaurants (which does not include any additional entertainment, such as movies). If we use the low figure of $30 per weekend, then she spends another $120 per month eating out on the weekend. That brings her grand total for eating out each month to $760!

She didn't even realize she was spending that much money so frivolously. As she gave me the numbers and I started multiplying them, she was shocked. That's why it's important to actually write it down: you can see it. If you never do this, you will not have a true appreciation for the amount of money being spent (and wasted).

Can this money be better used? Of course it can. Why eat up all your money eating out? If you think about it, you are literally flushing your money down the toilet. Wouldn't it be better to save that money so it can grow for you? The easy solution here is to bring your lunch from home. If you're too rushed in the morning, then prepare it the night before. I'm not saying don't ever eat out. But I am saying if you want to gain control of your finances, eating out shouldn't be a way of life. Save that money. Think about the woman in our example. How wonderful and productive it would be if she put that $760 a month into an IRA or emergency fund. Buy groceries that fill both needs—food for home and food for lunch. You will save money and you may eat healthier. Food prepared at home is normally healthier than restaurant food.

The key is to focus on things that benefit you, your family, and your finances now and into the future. Scale back on areas that are costing you money but adding little benefit or value to you and your family. Once you get to a place of properly managing your money, you can gradually add back a few of the things you may have to eliminate now (such as eating out, shopping, cable, or movies). Focus and discipline are critical.

As you go through the process of trying to reduce your expenses, you should also look at ways to increase your income. This is always a good idea! Is it time for a job change or to apply for a promotion? Can you find some part-time or side work? Should you invest time into switching into a higher-paying career? Always look to improve your skill set so you're in a position to be promoted or make a career change.

There can be more to balancing the M.I.M.O. equation than simply eliminating expenses. Work both sides of the equation to try to tip your balance to the surplus side and keep it there.

Managing Your Money by Balancing Your Checkbook

A big part of managing your money is keeping a balanced checkbook. Let's take a look at some easy steps to achieve this goal. If you haven't balanced your checkbook in a while, this may seem overwhelming. But I promise you it's quite simple once you make it a part of your routine. Easy as 1, 2, 3!

Here are the three steps to a balanced checkbook:

- **Step 1:** We need to verify your account entries first. Check your statement (either the hard copy or online) and verify all posted transactions. *Posted* means they are showing up on the bank's side on your statement. The transactions will include both debits and credits. Your debit transactions will be debit

A big part of managing your money is keeping a balanced checkbook.

card usage, checks, ATM withdrawals, and automatic debits to pay bills (bill pay). Don't forget fees. Your credit transactions are simply your deposits. Check off each transaction in your check register as you go down the list. If there are some transactions you haven't written in your register yet, go ahead and write them in. You need to account for each transaction. If you see transactions that are not familiar to you, check with your bank.

- **Step 2:** Look at the balance on your bank statement (the ending balance) and the corresponding date of the statement (normally at the top right). Compare the bank's ending balance to the balance in your checkbook on that same date. Make sure you match the dates. Do the figures match? If not, look for transactions that have not posted to your account yet (on the bank's side) or transactions you missed. You may also have transactions that occurred after the bank's ending statement date.

- **Step 3:** Either add or subtract the non-posted transactions from your balance as of the statement date. Add the amounts to the ending balance if the non-posted transactions are debits (withdrawals) from your account. You add debits to your figure for balancing purposes only because the money hasn't been taken from your account yet, so the bank's statement will show that money is still in your account. You know the money isn't there if you wrote a check, so don't try to re-spend it! Count it as gone. Subtract the amounts from the ending figure for balancing purposes if the non-posted transactions are credits (deposits) to your account. Subtract because the credit hasn't shown up yet so the bank will show those funds are not in your account. This should give you a checkbook balance that matches the bank's balance.

Easy as 1 2 3

Compare the bank's ending balance to the balance in your checkbook on that same date.

Let's look at an example to clarify things. Suppose the bank shows a $1,100 balance but I show a $1,000 balance in my checkbook. Well, I wrote a check for $100 that isn't showing up yet. The bank shows a balance of $1,100 since the $100 check hasn't been cashed yet. But I *know* the check was written so I know I don't have that $100. The check will eventually be cashed. If it's not cashed within a reasonable period of time, I can check with the person or business the check is written to. This was a simple example, but the same principle applies if there are multiple outstanding transactions.

Once you get your checkbook balanced, keep it balanced. Check your account at least once a week and make sure it balances. The more frequently you do this, the less time it will take. It will be quick and easy since there will be fewer transactions to monitor and calculate. I recommend once a day or once every other day. Make it a system. Make it a habit.

ALWAYS go directly to your checkbook after each transaction you make and write down the debit or credit. Keep a running total. Check it online versus what your check register shows. Developing and maintaining this habit sets you free and gives you a sense of accomplishment and pride.

Each time you balance your account, write "balance" on that line of your check register so you know the last date you balanced the account.

Each time you balance your account, write "balance" on that line of your check register so you know the last date you balanced the account. This is very helpful because it gives you a "last balance" date. If your figures are off the next time you're trying to balance your checkbook, you only need to go back to the last time you know you balanced your checkbook (your "last balance" date) to double-check figures (addition and subtraction). Also, place a circle (or asterisk) next to transactions that haven't posted yet so you can look for them on future reviews. This is very helpful because if you don't balance due to any non-posted transactions, you'll know why.

If the balances don't match, review your numbers and calculations again. If everything is done correctly and you still can't balance it, you may have to just make a one-time adjustment to your account (by adding or subtracting) because you may never be able to figure it out. This may be necessary if you haven't balanced your checkbook in a while (or ever!). I did that. I admit it. I just chalked it up to the past mistake of not continuing to monitor and balance my account and I made the adjustment. But now, I'm FREE! I balance every account to the penny every few days. It's a wonderful thing.

Budgeting

Once you have completed your cash flow analysis in worksheet 1, reviewed your M.I.M.O., and chosen some expenses to eliminate or reduce, you are well on your way to having a budget. If you are married, you and your spouse will obviously have to come to an agreement on these issues so you can achieve financial success.

> Review the last three months of your bank statements to see where your "budgeted money" is being spent.

The categories we used in the cash flow analysis will help you with budgeting. Live by spending only a certain amount of money in different categories: food, housing (including utilities), car note, insurance, retirement, savings, "reward money" (when applicable, spend on whatever!), and so forth. Review the last three months of your bank statements to see where your "budgeted money" is being spent. Between your cash flow analysis and your recent bank statements, you will have a clear understanding of your current spending. This will enable you to establish numbers for your budget.

For example, if you spend an average of $500 a month on food/groceries, make sure you budget to spend no more than $500 every month for the food/groceries category. I actually recommend rounding that figure down to make yourself economize and stay aware of how much money you are spending. Round it down to $450 and MAKE IT WORK!

Don't just try this with your groceries. Determine the "necessary" amount spent in the categories and try to decrease those amounts and stick with it. Stay within that allotted amount each month. DO NOT STRAY! Extra money can be added to "reward money" so that you feel the benefit, or it should be added to another category that needs shoring up (such as your emergency savings or your retirement account).

Hold each other accountable (or if you're single, try to partner with someone who is also financially disciplined to maintain consistency). The best advice I can give you is to manage your money. Don't let your money manage you.

Easy as 1 2 3

Stay within your allotted budget amounts each month. DO NOT STRAY!

If you have children, I recommend involving them in finances and budgeting as soon as they are old enough to understand. When you start giving them an allowance, you should begin to teach them basic concepts of money management—saving, budgeting, compound interest, and so forth. Children learn what they are taught and from what they observe, whether good or bad. Let's tilt the money-management scale in their favor. What they learn about money as children and teenagers will have a major impact on their lives. Are you helping them or hurting them?

No discussion of budgeting is complete without talking about credit. My point is a simple one: If you don't have the money to buy something, please don't buy it. Live within your means. If you follow this rule, you will save yourself much grief. Of course, I am talking about charging everyday purchases and consumer goods, such as groceries, dinner, movies, concerts, appliances, furniture, clothes, and so forth. I'm not saying that you shouldn't finance a home or a car. But I will say that you shouldn't stretch a car loan beyond three years. If you can't pay off the car in three years, then you can't afford the car. But aside from a car or a home, wait until you have the money to buy the item, then make the purchase.

I call credit card spending "fantasy money" because you're not using your own money to make the purchase. You're borrowing money. At the moment you make the purchase, you don't feel the effect of spending the money, which makes it an easy path to financial destruction. Using credit cards is like living in fantasyland because you're getting what you want but you're not aware of the cost. Think about it. When people are on drugs, they feel great for the moment; but when the high wears off, reality sets in. That isn't so pleasant. Reality hits when the credit card bill comes in. That will bring you back to earth. We know that drug use damages the physical body and mindset. Well, the continual use of credit cards damages your financial body and mindset. Go cold turkey and get off the credit card ride.

Easy as 1 2 3

You shouldn't stretch a car loan beyond three years. If you can't pay off the car in three years, then you can't afford the car.

I do realize that going cold turkey may work for some but not others. I strongly recommend this method though. Just realize you need to get off that merry-go-round and do it. But, if you need to come down off the high slowly, here are some steps you can take.

- **Month One**: Cut back on the number of charges. Look at your credit card statement and decide to use your credit card for only "two thirds" of the purchases you normally make. So, if your credit card statement has fifteen lines on it (charges) you will only charge ten items this month. When you do this, make sure you have accurately and truthfully completed the cash flow review AND reduced/eliminated some spending. Use the savings from the cash flow review to pay for the items you normally charge. Also, determine what items you can do without and don't purchase them. Do not purchase the items you can't afford to purchase with cash. Do without them. This first month will be tough but make a commitment to do it. I'm giving a little so you need to give a little. Telling you it's okay to charge is hurting me, but I am giving you a slow way out if you can't go cold turkey. Take the first baby step so you can get off the seemingly endless cycle of credit card debt.

Easy as 1 2 3

> Credit card spending is spending with fantasy money.

- **Month Two**: Cut back some more. Charge only one third of your normal purchases (five charges in our example). Repeat the cash flow review from month one and use savings to pay for more of your purchases instead of charging. Again, if you can't pay for the item(s) with cash, do not purchase them. Do without them. It should get a little easier on this step. You should have made some adjustments from month one so month two doesn't hurt so badly. It's a process. Hang in there.

- **Month Three**: No charging. By the third month you have had enough time to use savings from your cash flow analysis to pay in cash, change your mindset about charging, distinguish "needs" and "wants," and discover how to live on less. You will experience a true freedom when you receive a credit card bill that has no amount due!

A debit card is different. I call a debit card "reality money" because when you swipe the card to buy something, the money comes directly out of your account. Your bank account experiences an immediate consequence. If you swipe your debit card to make a $100 purchase, that money will come out of your account immediately. That's reality. This is another reason it's so important to keep your account balanced. You don't want to swipe the debit card and be charged overdraft fees because you had insufficient funds. And whatever you do, don't use the **SWAP** method— **SW**ipe And Pray!

Easy as 1 2 3

Whatever you do, don't use the **SWAP** method— **SW**ipe And Pray!

Maintaining a good credit history is essential in order to get good credit terms when you're trying to obtain a mortgage or a car loan. Be proactive at keeping a good credit score, which is a score each person is assigned based on their credit history. Lenders use a person's credit score to help determine if they think a person is a good risk. It's a judge of your trustworthiness, your character. The most important factor used to develop your credit score is your payment history. Please pay your bills on time. Late payments, charge-offs, and bankruptcies have a very negative affect on your credit score. People with poor credit pay more to borrow money than people with good credit. It's a simple fact. Why pay 20 percent for a car loan when you can pay 3 percent (or less) with good credit? Why pay twice the interest on a mortgage than someone with good credit?

Furthermore, many insurance companies use credit as a factor in the rates they charge. This element of developing an insurance rate has a drastic affect on a person's premiums. Many employers pull a person's credit before consideration for employment. Your credit affects more than your ability to borrow money at favorable terms. It affects your entire life. Why put yourself at a disadvantage?

Put yourself in the right position to get the best rates for various products and services. Give yourself a chance at that career opportunity instead of being denied right off the bat due to poor credit. Stay on top of your credit!

Easy as 1 2 3

The most important factor used to develop your credit score is your payment history.

Your credit score follows you wherever you go. You cannot escape it. Have you ever spoken with a person who has bad breath and you're just trying to evade the grasp of the smell? You hold your breath, turn your head, back away—anything to escape it. But no matter which direction you turn, that breath is all over you. It's inescapable! That's how your credit is. It's all over you. Try to make it a sweet aroma that welcomes people (lenders), not a funky smell that scares them away.

There are many websites that give helpful information on credit, your credit score, and so forth. Some of these websites are www.experian.com, www.transunion.com, and www.equifax.com. Cruise these sites and equip yourself with the information you need. You can order a free credit report from each of the above agencies once every twelve months. The official site to help consumers obtain a free credit report is www.annualcreditreport.com.

The topics discussed in this chapter are your foundation. They are the building blocks for your financial future. It may be cliché, but it's still true: without a solid foundation, your finances will crumble. You need to conquer the basics so you can move on to the next stage. There is no compromise on the basics: complete a cash flow analysis (M.I.M.O.), establish and maintain a budget, properly manage your money (balance your checkbook and so forth), and protect your credit. If you want to build financial success, you can't ignore the foundation.

I want to commend the first timers. I know it's tough. Take pride in the fact that you're heading in the right direction and that YOU WILL get control of your finances. Hey, I applaud people who weren't very successful the first time around (or second or third) and

have made a decision to give it another try. Money management is a mindset and an ongoing process. It takes determination, discipline and, often, sacrifice, but it is all worth it in the end. Look at the big picture. You may have to buckle down for the next six months, twelve months, or eighteen months. You will see some progress in the first few months, but this is a mere blip in time compared to the decades of financial freedom and financial success you will enjoy when you apply these concepts. Congratulations on taking this step!

Easy as 1 2 3

Easy as 1 2 3

Making Your Money Work for You

There is more to money management than simply paying the bills on time and putting money in a savings account. There are many plans to help you save and invest your money. Here are three questions to answer before you make decisions about saving and investing money:

1. What is the purpose of the money?
2. What is my time horizon?
3. What is my risk tolerance?

Your answers to these questions will help you place your money in the appropriate accounts. Each answer gives you an indication of how to use your money to your best advantage. Let's look at each question in greater detail.

The Purpose of the Money

Easy as 1 2 3

The purpose of the money will give you an idea of where to put your funds.

The purpose of the money will give you an idea of where to put your funds. If the purpose of the money is to save for retirement or for a young child's college fund, then you would place the funds in a much different plan than if the purpose of the money is to buy a home next year or shore up emergency savings.

Let me give you an example. A client called me and said he had a few hundred thousand dollars at his disposal, but he didn't know the best place to put it. The first thing I asked him was, "What do you want the money to do for you?" (In other words, the purpose of the money). He said he wanted to use it to buy some property in a few years.

In one sentence, he gave me the purpose (to buy property) and the time horizon (two years). With such a short time horizon I knew the client should be conservative with the money. He needed a safe place for this money, so a CD was the option he chose. The bank CD (certificate of deposit) guaranteed his principle and promised a certain locked percentage of interest on his money over the two-year period. We could have put the money in something that *may have* given him a higher return, but that would not have been wise. The chance of high returns always comes with more risk.

I have another client who calls me every time he has some extra money. He's an elderly gentleman, and he usually tells me he wants to put the money in the best place to benefit his daughter when he should pass. This is important information. If the money is purely to benefit his daughter when he passes, that makes a big difference in the types of plans he should be considering. If a person is not in tune with this or their advisor doesn't

The chance of high returns always comes with more risk.

ask the right questions the person can miss out on the best plan for him (or, in this case, his daughter).

Let's look at an example everyone can relate to. We all have bills to pay, so we all have money to be used for that purpose. That requires a checking account. However, you should not keep any "extra" money in your checking account. The only money you should have in your checking account is enough money to pay bills plus a little float money. If your bills total $2,000 a month, why would you keep $5,000 in your checking account (or even $3,000)? People do this all the time, and they shouldn't. Your money should always work for you. The extra money should be placed in an interest-bearing account (leave a little float money in there though, maybe $500). The extra money should intentionally be placed in an account that is for a specific purpose. Don't just let it sit there doing nothing for you with no purpose. Banks love it when you park money in an account and don't require them to pay you any interest on it. You better believe *they* are earning interest on your money. That's how a bank works. They use your money to make money. You should certainly make the bank pay you for using your money. Even earning low interest is better than no interest earned. Again, keeping the purpose of the money in mind is key.

If the purpose of the money is retirement, you should look into 401k plans, IRAs, and annuities. There is a wide range of retirement plans for you to choose from. If you're saving the money to use within the next five years or less, you should look into plans like CDs, savings accounts, or money market accounts. It may be tempting to be more aggressive with the money but you'll risk losing the money (or part of it) with too short of a window of time to recover the losses.

Easy as 1 2 3

If the purpose of the money is retirement, you should look into 401k plans, IRAs, and annuities.

Keep in mind that different types of products have different tax consequences. Some accounts are taxable, some are tax deferred, and some are tax free. Each is an option for most people. To help us better understand the impact of these possibilities, let's equate the taxable status to the concept of your parents chastising you when you were a child (or how you discipline your children as a parent now). A taxable account has no tax advantages. You take the tax hit on any growth every year. This is like your parents punishing you for something you did wrong; there is no lenience. Just take it. A tax deferred account allows you to get away with not paying taxes currently, but you're gonna pay the piper later, in full. This is similar to your parents telling you that you're going to get it later. That's a tense wait! But a tax-free account let's you get off scot-free. No taxes on the growth of your account! Sweet. That's like your parents saying, "Okay, no punishment. You got off this time." Which do you like best?

Believe it or not, the vast majority of people qualify for accounts that grow tax deferred with growth that can be withdrawn "tax free." It all goes back to the purpose of the money. You must use the money in these accounts for the intended purpose to reap the tax-free benefit.

The accounts are not a big secret, but many people just aren't aware of them. A Roth IRA is meant for retirement, a Coverdell Education Savings Account is meant for education, and a 529 Plan is also meant for education. There are income limitations for the Roth IRA and Coverdell ESA, but most people earn below these limits. Speak with a financial advisor to determine which plans best fit your situation.

Easy as 1 2 3

Some accounts are taxable, some are tax deferred, and some are tax free. Each is an option for most people.

Your Time Horizon

Your time horizon is merely the amount of time you plan to save/invest the money. You do not plan to use the money during this time. If you don't plan to use the money for twenty years, then your time horizon is twenty years. The longer your time horizon, the more aggressive you may want to be with the money to take advantage of time and compound interest (earning interest on top of interest). However, a more aggressive account will come with more risk. It's also important to note that there may be penalties for withdrawing the money early. For that reason, it's important that you don't invest money you might possibly need in the short-term in a long-term investment product. Carefully consider your needs and your time horizons.

Take advantage of long time horizons to the degree that you can. You cannot re-live time or regain what is lost. It's best to take advantage of it early. A person who starts saving money at age twenty will have substantially more money saved at age sixty-five than a person who waits until age thirty or forty to start saving (given the same amount of monthly contributions and same interest rate earned). This is due to time and the concept of compound interest.

Let me show you an example. Let's say John started saving $500 a month ($6,000 a year) at age twenty. Let's say he does this for forty-five years and earns 8 percent compound interest. How much do you think he'll have at age sixty-five when he chooses to retire? The operative word here is *chooses*. You want to have the option to choose to retire when you want to instead of needing to work until age eighty-five because you never saved for retirement. Think ahead. Give yourself options through proper planning. That's what John did. Because he started saving at age twenty, his total will equal more than $2.3 million at age sixty-five! Amazing right? Do you see what I mean now? He only contributed $270,000 but the beauty of compound interest over time worked in his favor. Start early!

Let's look at Beth who decided to wait until age thirty to start saving her $500 per month ($6,000 a year). Beth is going to earn the same 8 percent compound interest on her money but she only has thirty-five years to save. It doesn't seem like much of a time difference right? It's only ten years. Well, ten years means a lot in the world of compound interest. Beth will have a drastically lower amount at age sixty-five than John. Beth's retirement savings will equal a little over $1 million. This is less than half of John's nest egg. Get the picture? John started early and he is benefiting from it.

How about Bill who waits until age forty to start saving? He starts contributing his $500 a month for retirement ($6,000 a year) but he only has twenty-five years to save. He will earn 8 percent

Easy as 1 2 3

Don't invest money you might possibly need in the short-term in a long-term investment product.

compound interest too, but for only twenty-five years. His total will equal just under $440,000. Bill's total is less than half of Beth's retirement account. Bill had ten years less than Beth to save and twenty years less than John. Time is crucial. This has to hit you over your head like a brick. Please start early. I come across clients all the time who say, "I wish I'd known then what I know now. I would have done things differently." Learn from their experience! You can't make up lost time.

The longer your time horizon, the more aggressive you may want to be with the money to take advantage of time and compound interest (earning interest on top of interest).

On the other hand, a shorter time horizon should yield a more conservative approach to handling your money. You have less time to recover from losses so it's best to reign in the level of aggression as time draws near to use the money. Be realistic and take the time to figure out how long you really want to keep the account going without touching it.

Your Risk Tolerance

Your risk tolerance is basically your willingness to take a chance with your money. Aggressive investors are willing to take a bigger risk with their money to try to achieve more growth. Moderate investors are willing to take a risk to achieve more growth but don't want to be too risky. Conservative investors are not willing to take much risk with their money; instead, they want to make sure they keep what they have and they are not as concerned with growth. There is no right or wrong answer about risk tolerance. Each person has his or her own comfort level. Decide for yourself.

Seek wise and knowledgeable counsel before putting your money somewhere. This is important.

Each person should feel comfortable with the way their money is being handled. If you get ulcers when the stock market goes through some turmoil, make sure your assets are invested according to your risk tolerance so you can sleep in peace. Use reason when making this decision and be real with yourself. It's your money, and it's your decision. Don't be guided by emotion, but do your research and apply logic and rational thinking. You don't have to know it all, but you should have a clue about some things. There's a wealth of information available on the Internet and in books. Educate yourself, but don't let that be the end of your due diligence.

Easy as 1 2 3

Your risk tolerance is your willingness to take a chance with your money.

My advice to anyone is to speak with someone who is knowledgeable about handling money and dealing with people's finances. The person should be familiar with money management and the scope of financial products that fit different situations. Make sure the person is knowledgeable and trustworthy. These are two character traits you definitely want in a person who is helping you manage your finances.

Educating yourself about financial products and options and seeking wise counsel should be an ongoing process. These actions will help you to make the best decisions for your financial future and avoid getting scammed, which we will talk about next.

Don't Get Scammed

Before we get into some details about good ways to use and invest your money, please allow me to give you some words of wisdom.

If something sounds too good to be true, it probably is too good to be true. Please don't get caught up in get-rich-quick schemes. Over the years people have told me about various schemes, businesses, and high-return investments—but there is always a catch. Do not be deceived! Follow a sound, logical plan that allows you to build wealth over time. Be careful with any product, business, or idea that promises quick and/or high returns. Don't get taken.

Easy as 1 2 3

Educating yourself about financial products and options and seeking wise counsel should be an ongoing process.

One individual called to tell me about a product his wife was told would guarantee them a 10 percent return over ten years. I advised him that was highly unlikely and to be wary. I told him I'd review the information for him and said if it checked out, I would put some money in it! Of course, I never received the information.

If someone approaches you with an opportunity that sounds too good to be true or promises a high return with a low- to no-risk product, I recommend you take the following steps:

1. Ask for the information in writing. Tell the salesperson you would like to have any brochures or pamphlets that give details about the product so you can review it. If the person can't give you anything in writing, you should not even entertain their pitch. DO NOT BUDGE on this. Get it in writing on official company documents, pamphlets, or brochures.

2. Tell the person you will take the information home and review it. Let the person know you will give them a call if you're interested or if you have any questions. There may be

a pressure tactic employed at that point. DO NOT BUDGE on this. DO NO GET PRESSURED. The deal won't be gone tomorrow or next week or next month. If it's legitimate, it will be around after you've had time to check it out.

If something sounds too good to be true, it probably is too good to be true.

3. Review the information with some people you trust. If you're married, you definitely should consult your spouse first. You may want to prepare a list of questions to discuss with some trusted advisors as well as with the person advocating the product.

4. Use the Internet to check out the company and the product. Online reviews can be quite helpful; just beware that sometimes companies post their own "reviews" of their products.

5. Once you've gathered all your "facts" and discussed the opportunity with some trusted advisors, you'll be ready to make a decision about the product's legitimacy and whether it's right for you.

If you follow these steps, you should be able to avoid getting trapped in an illegitimate scheme. I had to mention get-rich-quick schemes because many people fall for these schemes and never get their money back. It's a terrible shame because their hard-earned money is lost forever. I don't want that to happen to you, and I know you don't either. Stay away from this type of "wealth building." Be patient. Use wise judgment. Exercise discipline.

Now let's turn our attention to the kind of accounts and plans that can help you manage your money and build your wealth.

Savings Account

I recommend you open two different savings accounts. One savings account should be for emergencies and the other one should be for known future expenses. I call it a "slush fund."

Remember, always keep non-bill-paying money in interest-bearing accounts. You want your money to be in interest-bearing mode as much as possible.

Your emergency savings account should have three to six months of your monthly living expenses in it. You can get this figure from the cash flow analysis worksheet in chapter one. Three months is the minimum, but six months is ideal in most cases. If you don't have that much money in your account now, don't panic. You have to start somewhere.

Open an account, start contributing to it, and keep contributing to it until you reach that goal. Something is better than nothing. If you contribute $50 per week, which would give you $200 a month, then your account will have $2,400 after one year. And so on. It's better to have something in the account than nothing. Even if you only put away $25 a week, you'll end up with over $1,200 in a year. Zero dollars covers nothing, but $2,400 (or $1,200) will cover a lot of emergencies.

The "slush fund" savings account is an account that will help ease your mind for those big ticket items that come up every year — vacation, Christmas, family reunion, taxes, tuition, and so forth. That's

Easy as 123

Always keep non-bill-paying money in interest-bearing accounts.

what planning is for. You know these big-ticket expenses come up every year so why not plan for them? Determine how much each of these categories adds up to, then divide the total figure by twelve. That's how much you should contribute to this savings account each month so you have the funds available when those expenses arise.

Easy as 1 2 3

Saving some money is better than saving nothing.

For instance, suppose you need $1,000 for vacation, $500 for Christmas, $600 for your family reunion, $400 for birthdays, and $500 for your anniversary. These expenses add up to $3,000. If we divide $3,000 by twelve, that equals $250 per month. That is the amount that should be contributed to the slush fund account each month.

I have done this for years, and it gives me such a feeling of freedom. This is "managing your money." I assure you that you will feel much better knowing the funds are available for these expenses instead of wondering where the money is going to come from or having to resort to a credit card. Plan ahead. Don't get stuck wondering how you'll afford Christmas or birthday presents.

CDs and Money Market Accounts

Accounts like these may allow you to gain a higher rate of interest than an ordinary savings account. A CD (certificate of deposit) locks in an interest rate for a certain period of time. The minimum to open a CD (which may be $1,000 or $500, depending on your institution) is normally greater than the amount needed to open a savings account. CDs carry a penalty for early withdrawal, so it is ideal to keep the funds in the CD for the entire period of time (one year, two years, whatever it may be). A CD is ideal if you want to protect your principal in the short term, earn a guaranteed rate of interest, and know you don't need the funds for a definite period of time (one year, two years, whatever the case may be). Your principal will be FDIC insured up to $250,000 (through December 31, 2013), and the bank will guarantee a certain rate of interest during the CD's term. FDIC protection will return to $100,000 on January 1, 2014, except IRAs and some other retirement accounts. They will remain at $250,000.

A money market account doesn't lock in the interest rate but normally provides a higher interest rate than a typical savings account. These accounts usually allow some limited check-writing privileges as well. Money market accounts may require a higher minimum to open an account as well as a higher minimum monthly balance.

The money market account is better if you want to stay liquid and not lock up your money into a CD. You may want the money safe but also want unlimited access to it in the short term. FDIC protection up to $250,000 applies to these accounts too as already noted.

Look at the details when considering these accounts.

Easy as 1 2 3

Plan ahead and put money into a slush fund each month for birthdays, vacation, Christmas, and other big-ticket expenses. Don't get stuck wondering how you'll afford Christmas or birthday presents.

Retirement Account

Everyone should save for retirement because the odds are high that you'll make it to retirement. I say this because I've had some people say, "What if I don't make it to retirement? I may die tomorrow, so I live for today." It is true. You should enjoy today because you never know what will happen tomorrow. You could be hit by a bus tomorrow! Nevertheless, my answer to these people is, "Well, what if you *do* make it to retirement?" If you lived your life like there was no tomorrow and didn't prepare or save for the future that would make you BROKE! (As well as a little silly and irresponsible.) I won't say what I really want to say, but let's just say it doesn't make you the sharpest knife in the drawer.

Easy as 1 2 3

If your company matches your contributions in their retirement plan, you really should contribute to the plan to get the FREE MONEY!

There are plenty of ways to save for retirement. There are retirement plans through work and there are IRAs. There are even plans available for self-employed people and business owners. Start early. Put something away. You can start out small and increase your contributions as you are able. This should be a major priority.

If your company matches your contributions in their retirement plan, you really should contribute to the plan to get the FREE MONEY! Seriously. If you're not contributing to this matching plan, then you are giving away money. Who does that? Make the sacrifice and contribute at least the amount your company matches. I doubt you'll even feel it, but your retirement account will definitely feel it!

Some people think they don't need to save for retirement because they will get Social Security. Unfortunately, Social Security is not enough to retire on. Furthermore, the Social Security program is in major trouble. Please read the front page of your Social Security statement for additional details. You're in for a major revelation if you haven't done this before. I'll give you a sneak peek of some of the high-lights.

The front page of my Social Security statement is identical to yours. The only difference is the name and address. Here are some important excerpts:

Easy as 1 2 3

Retirement savings trump education savings because there is no such thing as a retirement loan, retirement grant, or retirement scholarship.

- "...Social Security was never intended to be your only source of income when you retire. You also will need other savings, investments, pensions or retirement accounts to make sure you have enough money to live comfortably when you retire..."

- "...the Social Security system is facing serious financial problems..."

- "...In 2017 we will begin paying more in benefits than we collect in taxes. Without changes, by 2041 the Social Security Fund will be exhausted..."

Is that clear enough for you? Prioritize retirement savings. If you have to decide between retirement savings and education savings due to income or budget restraints, choose retirement savings. Yes, retirement savings trump education savings. I know you want to save for your child's education and help them in that endeavor, but your children can get loans, grants, or scholarships. There is no such thing as a retirement loan, retirement grant, or retirement scholarship.

Look at it this way. You're doing yourself, your children, and your grandchildren a great service by making retirement savings a priority. You don't want to be a burden to your children or grandchildren by having to borrow from them because you have no money to retire on. Your children will have their own families and responsibilities at that time. Be smart. Save for your retirement. You'll be glad you did.

Let me give you a quick, easy way to understand how much money you may need at retirement. This is very simplified, but it gives you an idea of what to think about. First, at what age do you plan to retire? For this example, let's say age sixty-five. Second, how long do you expect to be in retirement? In other words, how long do you expect to live? Let's choose age one hundred. Hey, don't laugh or scoff. I plan to live to age 105 or 110! But, for you, we'll say age one hundred. That's thirty-five years in retirement. Third, how much money do you think you'll need each year while in retirement? Hopefully, you'll enter retirement debt free, so you'll only have basic bills (such as food, utilities, gas, and so forth). You want to account for extras like travel, grandchildren (spoiling them), and other gratuitous spending too. Let's say you can live comfortably on $40,000 a year ($3,333 per month). Next, how long do you have to save? We'll say you're thirty years old, so you have thirty-five years to save until you're sixty-five. Remember, starting earlier is better because it gives you more time to accumulate compound interest.

Finally, let's get to the basic math. Thirty-five years in retirement times $40,000 a year equals $1.4 million needed by age sixty-five. We aren't going to get complicated and go into the fact that $1.4 million today will really need to be almost $4 million in thirty-five years—since the average rate of inflation is a little over 3 percent. We're going to use the $1.4 million figure. If you know you need $1.4 million by age sixty-five to live comfortably when you retire, what should you do? You should plan for it of course. Let's see how much you may need to save to reach your goal of $1.4 million.

To find out how much *you* will need to save, you need to use a financial calculator or you can go onto a website that calculates compound interest for you. There are numerous retirement calculators online that can walk you through this process, and a simple search should enable you to find a good one. I'll give you some figures here to finish out the example:

> Easy as 1 2 3
>
> More time to save and more interest earned equals more money accumulated to enjoy! Don't stick your head in the ground and ignore the obvious. You must save to have savings.

- If you save $8,200 a year for thirty-five years earning 8 percent compound interest, you'll reach $1.4 million. To do that, you'll need to save about $683 a month.

- If you only earn 6 percent compound interest, you'll have to save about $12,600 a year. That will mean saving $1,050 a month.

- If you do great and earn 10 percent compound interest per year, you'll only have to save $5,200 a year, or approximately $433 per month.

As you can see, time and the rate of compound interest earned are the major factors. The more time you have to save, the less you have to save each month and the less interest you have to earn to meet your goal. The less time you have to save, the more money you'll have to save each month and/or the more interest you'll have to earn.

More time to save and more interest earned equals more money accumulated to enjoy! Don't stick your head in the ground and ignore the obvious. You must save to have savings.

One of the easiest ways to prioritize this is to set up an automatic debit for your retirement savings so you don't have to remember to contribute to your account. Furthermore, an automatic debit eliminates the chance to reconsider. I recommend this for other savings accounts too. Make it automatic. Once you set up the automatic debits, it will be a debit you'll get used to. After a while you won't even miss the money. But the money will be put away growing for you.

Easy as 1 2 3

One of the easiest ways to prioritize retirement savings is to set up an automatic debit for your retirement savings so you don't have to remember to contribute to your account.

Education Savings Account

If you have some extra coins to spare, by all means save for your children's education. A college education can be expensive, and I'm sure you and your children will appreciate any amount set aside to offset some (or all) of these costs. The key is to use the proper type of accounts for college savings. Take advantage of tax qualified plans (the Coverdell Education Savings Account and 529 Plans) because these plans are designed to help you take advantage of growing your savings with no taxes on the gain as long as it's used for the intended purpose of education. There are also prepaid tuition plans. Speak with a financial professional to see what will work best for you.

Keeping in mind our discussion of time and compound interest, it is obviously best to start early. As soon as the child is born, you should open a college savings account if you are financially able. I've had many clients come to me a year or two before their child is about to graduate from high school. What can you accumulate that late? If you start early, you're ahead of the game.

If you start saving $100 a month ($1,200 a year) when a child is first born and you earn 8 percent annual return on the account, the total will be almost $45,000 when the child turns eighteen years old. If the account earns 6 percent, the total in the account will be around $37,000. A $200 monthly contribution ($2400 a year) basically doubles the total. A $50 monthly contribution cuts the total in half. Something saved is better than nothing saved.

Easy as 1 2 3

Use the proper type of tax-qualified plans for college savings. Speak with a financial professional to see what will work best for you.

Children and Savings

I recommend you involve your children in money management as soon as you start giving them money. If they understand the concept of spending money, they surely can grasp the concepts of saving money and managing money. This may be one of the greatest gifts you'll give them — the gift of understanding how to manage money. Open a starter account for each child and teach them basic concepts like how to balance their account, how interest is earned, and so forth. They'll be amazed to see their money growing and earning interest as it is left to accumulate.

Here's another great tip. When your children start earning income, open a Roth IRA for each of them. This will give them a huge head start on a retirement account. Let me give you an example. Let's say your child earned $5,000 a year from fifteen to eighteen years old. Put that money into a Roth IRA. Well, you know your child isn't going to want to put all their money in the IRA, so strike a deal and match their contributions. You contribute $2,500, and your child contributes $2,500. Since you've read this book, you've taught your children the importance of saving for the future and properly managing money so this won't be a new concept for them.

Easy as 1 2 3

Get your children involved in money management as soon as you start giving them money.

If a child invests $5,000 over four years, earning 8 percent compound interest, the account will be worth about $22,530. The interest earned doesn't appear that great in the short term ($2,530). Yet what if the money remains there to grow with no further contributions? If the money continues to grow for forty-seven years at 8 percent compound interest until the child reaches age sixty-five, the account will be worth well over $800,000! Now, that's what I call a head start.

Guess how much your child will owe in taxes on that money? Nothing! Tax-free growth applies to the Roth IRA as long as it is held at least five years and until age fifty-nine-and-a-half. The $20,000 investment (of after-tax money) ends up being worth over $800,000 by age sixty-five. That's great, but being able to access this account with over $780,000 in tax-free growth is beyond great—it's awesome! Are you loving this yet?

Miscellaneous Investments

There are countless vehicles for investing your money, including mutual funds, real estate, annuities, individual stocks, bonds. Each investment fits a different need. Do your research and get advice if you need to. A full discussion of these vehicles is beyond the scope of this book, but good advice is readily available. Enlist the help of a financial planning professional. Make sure you research the investment and know what you're getting into. Look at the positives and negatives, and don't invest in anything that doesn't fit your particular needs.

Easy as 1 2 3

When your children start earning income, open a Roth IRA for each of them. This will give them a huge head start on a retirement account.

Easy as 1 2 3

Easy as 1 2 3

Protecting Your Assets and Lifestyle

Now that we've addressed budgeting your money and using your money, let's move on to protecting your money. The idea of protecting your money is so important because the future is uncertain. Life just happens. You need to have some sense of security to remain sane!

I like to say that whatever your future plans may be, you definitely need a P.A.L. Your P.A.L. sticks with you through thick and thin. Your P.A.L. protects you and supports you. A true P.A.L. is there always. Life would be much more difficult if your P.A.L. wasn't around or if you had no P.A.L. at all. I think we all agree with this.

The P.A.L. I'm referring to is a plan to Protect Assets and Lifestyle. This P.A.L. takes the relationship to a whole new level—a level that delivers for you and provides for you in a time of need. People who have financial problems or have had financial problems can often trace their problems back to the loss or absence of a P.A.L. Those who have had their P.A.L. by their side during a loss or a setback can attest to the benefits of having their P.A.L. around.

Whatever your future plans may be, you definitely need a **P.A.L.**— a plan to **P**rotect your **A**ssets and **L**ifestyle.

Acquiring riches and possessions is one thing, but protecting them is another. After you have worked, budgeted, saved, and invested, how do you keep your money from disappearing? Before you celebrate the rewards of your labor, you should put a plan in place—your P.A.L.—to protect what you have accumulated.

Let me give you some examples of how your P.A.L. comes into play and helps preserve you, your family, your finances, and your stuff.

- If you need surgery (or are sick/injured and in need of medical treatment), what P.A.L. is going to come to your aid and take the financial hit for you? Health insurance.

- If you become disabled or sick and unable to work, what P.A.L. will step in for you and keep the cash flowing into the home so you can continue to pay your bills? Disability insurance.

- When an emergency arises (notice I said *when* not *if*), what P.A.L. can you turn to for help to bail you out? Emergency savings.

- If you are driving along, minding your business, and happen to slide into another car (or person), what P.A.L. do you call for assistance in paying the financial consequences (vehicle damage, injuries, death, lawsuit)? Auto insurance.

Make sure your protection keeps pace with your financial growth and responsibilities.

- If you or a loved one need long-term medical assistance due to physical and/or mental limitations from an accident, illness or other medical situation, what P.A.L. will show up and provide financial help to allow for proper care (control and options)? Long-term care insurance.

- If your home suffered damage due to any of the many things that can happen to it (fire, smoke, windstorm, burglary, hail, broken pipe, vandalism, weight of snow or ice, and so forth), where would you turn to for help? Homeowners insurance.

- If you are being sued for something you are liable for (or something you're not liable for—you still have to defend yourself and pay defense costs), how will you afford excellent counsel to defend you? Liability insurance.

- What will happen if your business is affected by a fire or a break in? What if a virus infects your business's computer system? What if someone sues your business because of faulty work or because of injuries to someone? Is there a P.A.L. that can get you out of this jam? Business insurance.

Easy as 1 2 3

- Who can your family rely on if you were to prematurely die? How will the mortgage be paid? How will your income be replaced? How will your children pay for college? How will your family continue their standard of living? How will your final expenses be paid? How will the car note, credit card bill, and other bills be paid without your income? Do you plan to leave a legacy that lives on even after you're gone? Life insurance.

Always have your P.A.L. in place to provide real protection for the things and people you value and the circumstances you face every day. Pay a little to protect a lot.

The list could go on and on. The purpose of your P.A.L. is to protect your assets and lifestyle. Why would you want to have a bunch of stuff and nothing to protect it? That is not wise. People with a lot of stuff (money, property, even fame) have a lot of protection, a P.A.L. Make sure your protection keeps pace with your financial growth and responsibilities.

Our first step is to make sure we always have our P.A.L. in place to provide real protection for the things and people we value and the circumstances we face every day. The concept here is to "pay a little to protect a lot." If I wanted to get really crazy with acronyms, I'd call this my P.A.L. P.A.L. theory, pay a little (P.A.L.), protect a lot (P.A.L.). Sorry, I couldn't let the opportunity pass me by. The small amount you pay each month provides you a lot of protection. For example, your homeowners policy may cost you $1,000 a year, but it provides hundreds of thousands of dollars in protection.

Easy as 1 2 3

Another P.A.L principle: "Pay a little to protect a lot."

You likely noticed that the common theme in most of the solutions we looked at revolves around insurance. Emergency savings isn't insurance per se, but it definitely comes in handy when an emergency arises. It is truly a P.A.L. Just remember that a suit or dress that is on sale is not an emergency. The old school principle "Save for a rainy day" applies here. The rainy day is the emergency.

Let's take a closer look at the P.A.L.s you need to see you through.

Health Insurance

Health insurance may be expensive, but you can't afford not to have it. If you become sick or get injured, it's much more expensive *not* to have health insurance. For that reason, health insurance shouldn't be on the list of expendable expenses if you're looking for ways to cut expenses. There are few things more important than health insurance because that's the only thing that will help you when you need to have surgery or receive other treatment.

Life happens. No one expects accidents, injuries, diseases, surgery, or treatment, but everyone should plan for it. Sometimes the visit to a doctor or hospital is inexpensive, but more often it is costly. Health insurance will help subsidize all, most, or much of the cost.

Here's a simple example. I tore my Achilles tendon several years ago while playing basketball with some colleagues. I guess I was trying a little too hard to be like Mike. Maybe I'll get a chance to play a pick up game with President Obama one day! Wouldn't that be great? Well, by the time it was all said and done, the cost for surgery, follow-up visits, and physical therapy was about $20,000. I didn't pay $20,000. I only paid my deductible and a small co-insurance amount. My health insurance paid the remainder. Your deductible is the amount you're responsible for before the insurance will start paying. For example, if you have a $500 deductible and your hospital bill is $5,000, you will be responsible for the first $500 while your insurance company will be responsible for the remaining $4,500. Some plans have co-insurance too. Co-insurance is your share of the remaining payment. To return to the example of the $5,000 bill, let's say you have an 80/20 co-insurance clause. This means your health insurance company pays 80 percent of the remaining bill and you pay 20 percent. So, you'd pay your $500 deductible plus $900 of coinsurance (20 percent of $4,500). In this example, you'd pay $1,400 of a $5,000 bill. Most insurance plans have a maximum amount you pay "out of pocket," then the insurance company pays 100 percent thereafter.

Easy as 1 2 3

Health insurance may be expensive, but you can't afford not to have it.

This is a mild example. Healthcare costs can be astronomical and cause major financial problems when this P.A.L. isn't around. Many people have to file bankruptcy because this P.A.L. was ignored or undervalued. Don't be another statistic. Look at higher deductibles and co-payments if you need to make the plan more affordable, but don't disregard health insurance. Appreciate this P.A.L. and make sure this P.A.L. is always by your side.

Disability Insurance

This P.A.L. protects your income earning ability in case of an injury or the onset of an illness that prevents you from working. If your income decreases or disappears, how will you pay your bills? Bills do not fluctuate with your income. In other words, your bills don't decrease just because your income decreases. Your bills will continue to arrive, and they will need to be paid. As a matter of fact, you'll probably have some new bills (hospital, doctor, physical therapist, and so forth) to treat the illness or injury — so your bills will likely increase! Disability protection will provide income to you while you recover from your illness or injury so you can continue to pay your bills.

> Disability insurance protects your income earning ability in case of an injury or the onset of an illness that prevents you from working.

If you are battling in your mind about the cost, think of it this way. Your cable bill is $50 or $100 a month, right? How many other costly "extras" do you spend money on every month? If you become disabled, what will you receive from the cable company each month? That's right. You'll receive a bill every month. But if you had a disability policy, what would you receive? You'd receive a check every month. See the difference? One continues to be a bill or a burden and the other turns into a benefit or help. The cost is minimal but the benefit is great.

Disability insurance is designed to pay 50-70 percent of a person's wages while they suffer a qualifying disability that renders the person unable to work. Policies come with various options. The benefit period (the pay-out period) can range widely, depending on the policy you choose. The elimination period, which is like a deductible, ranges widely too. The elimination period means the company will not pay anything out during this period of 30, 60, 90, 180, 365 days. A cost of living adjustment rider (an inflation rider to increase benefit amount) is usually available. See a professional to discuss the options that fit your needs.

Easy as 1 2 3

Bills do not fluctuate with your income.

I remember a client who I repeatedly advised to obtain disability income protection. Like many young and healthy people, she felt invincible. Well, she hobbled into my office one day after she sprained her knee playing flag football. She realized how bad it could have been. She is the sole wage earner and owns a home. Something as simple as an injury from a recreational activity could have caused her major financial problems. She has disability coverage now.

Another client told me she doesn't know how she would have made it without the disability check that paid her mortgage while she was going through breast cancer treatment.

Yet another client used her disability income policy to help pay her bills while she was on bed rest for most of her pregnancy. Yes, even a complication during pregnancy can be considered a disability. I hope you can see that disability insurance is a P.A.L. you can't afford to live without.

Emergency Savings

You should keep three to six months of your living expenses in a safe account backed by the FDIC (Federal Deposit Insurance Corporation). This P.A.L. allows you to respond to emergencies without greatly disrupting your finances or your life. This can be used for a lost job too. It will allow you time to seek new employment while meeting your financial obligations. Some simple planning can help you avoid or lessen obstacles that come down the road later.

People often get discouraged when they see that they should have three to six months of living expenses saved, because either they don't have that amount saved or they don't have anything saved. Don't be discouraged. Start saving now. The account will build up over time. Something in the account is better than nothing in the account.

An emergency savings account allows you to respond to emergencies without greatly disrupting your finances or your life.

Protect your sanity. Protect your credit. Protect yourself. Build up this P.A.L. so he's big and strong enough to help you in times of financial emergency.

Auto Insurance

Most of us ride with this P.A.L. every day. This P.A.L. provides broad protection for you and others as you drive your vehicle. You are protected from physical damage to your car, theft of your car, injuries to you and the passengers in your car, damages to someone else's car, injuries to others, and damage to a rental car. You spend a lot of time with this P.A.L. and don't even realize it. Some of you know this P.A.L. better than others because you've had to call on him on more than one occasion!

Many states require at least a minimum amount of coverage if you have your vehicle tagged. The state normally requires you to carry liability coverage to provide payment to others if you're at fault in causing damage to others' property, injuries to others, or death of others. States that require liability coverage will often fine you if you don't maintain the required coverage. Why waste that money by paying it to the state? Keep the policy in force at all times. Do not let it lapse.

Consider a few scenarios if you let your policy lapse. What if you total someone's car and injure the driver? Worse yet, what if the driver dies? You will be in a very bad position. Or what if you total your car while it's still being financed? Who's going to pay the bank? Not the insurance company if you let the policy lapse. You will still owe the bank thousands of dollars on a vehicle that doesn't exist because you didn't do something as simple as keep your auto policy in force. That's not smart, but I've seen it happen.

Easy as 1 2 3

Keep your auto insurance policy in force at all times. Do not let it lapse. You should carry more than the minimum automobile liability limits on your auto insurance policy. "Minimal limits" give you "minimal coverage."

Since we're on the topic, I'd like to strongly encourage you to make sure you are carrying adequate liability limits on your vehicle(s). Minimum automobile liability limits should not be carried. "Minimal limits" give you "minimal coverage." What happens if you have a "more than minimal" claim? If you cause $30,000 of damage but only have $15,000 of liability coverage, there is a problem. It doesn't cost much more to increase your limits to a reasonable level. You'll be glad you paid that extra $10 or $15 a month if you get involved in a more than minimal claim.

You should speak with your auto insurance carrier and ask for their advice on the limits and coverages that should be carried in your state. Different states have different requirements.

Long-Term Care Insurance

People are living longer these days, but they are not necessarily able to take care of themselves in their later years. The cost of this care is alarming and should be carefully planned for before the need arises. You may not believe it, but there is a 50 percent chance that you will need this kind of protection plan at some point — and it may be sooner than you think. Forty percent of people who need long-term care services are working adults under age sixty-five, so it's not for seasoned clients only.

According to U.S. Census data, the national average cost for long-term care is $75,000 a year.

According to U.S. Census data, the national average cost for long-term care is $75,000 a year. That's over $6,000 a month! Do you have that kind of money? Your P.A.L. can absorb most or all of the costs associated with these services with a little planning. Early planning to obtain a policy costs a small fraction of what these services would cost you in the end. Plans range in cost based on age and health, but generally they cost between $50 to $200-plus per month. If you're young and healthy, you can lock in a good rate. It's better than waiting until the time comes and having to exhaust your assets (retirement, savings, home) to pay for the care you need. Obtain coverage while you're younger and healthy to lock in a lower rate. Remember: pay a little to protect a lot.

There are a wide range of reasons people require long-term care services, including automobile accidents, stroke, and disabling diseases (such as multiple sclerosis, Parkinson's disease, and Alzheimer's disease). I remember inspecting a client's property one day to write a policy on their home. I went down to the client's basement and there was a man in his twenties laid up in a hospital bed being cared for by a custodial caregiver. I asked what happened and she explained he was shot in the neck. He was paralyzed from the neck down. This is tragic, but it's an example of one of many things that can happen to put a person in the position of needing this type of coverage.

Easy as 1 2 3

Obtain long-term care coverage while you're young and healthy to lock in a lower rate.

You might also consider buying a plan for your parents if they can't afford it. Think about it. If they can't afford long-term care insurance, they certainly can't afford long-term care. Who do you think will be paying the cost if they don't have the resources? You will. Again, do you have $6,000 to $10,000 a month to provide long-term care services for your parents? It would be wise to proactively think of a way to help solve this dilemma — to plan ahead. If you have siblings (or other relatives), get them to chip in so it's less of a cost to each person. I strongly encouraged my parents to obtain coverage. Fortunately my mom is able to pay her own premium. If not, I'd be more than happy to pay her $60 a month premium to avoid paying $6,000 to $10,000 a month later. No brainer.

I obtained long-term care protection for myself when I was fairly young (in my thirties). I told a client about this as I was writing her plan. My innocent comment prompted a friendly debate. She said I was wasting my money by purchasing a long-term care policy at such a young age. This client is sharp, but I had to challenge her on this. She was about sixty-five at the time. I asked her to find a sheet of paper and a pen and explained to her what my rate would be for the same policy she was purchasing. As a thirty-year-old male in preferred condition, I would pay less than $80/month. I explained that if I paid $80/month for thirty-five years (to age sixty-five, the client's current age), I would have paid $33,600 for the coverage over that time frame. Then we looked at how much she was paying. By age sixty-five, the policy is much more expensive *and* you may not qualify for a preferred rate due to some

Easy as 1 2 3

Consider buying a long-term care plan for your parents if they can't afford it.

ailment (that comes with age and time). Her rate was over $350/month (more than four times my rate). That's over $4,200 a year. So she will pay more in eight years for the same coverage than I would pay in thirty-five years. (I divided my thirty-five-year payout in premium of $33,600 by her annual premium of $4,200 to reach that answer.) After she reviewed the numbers, she agreed I was making a wise decision.

Why wait until it's more expensive or you're more prone to be ineligible due to some health reason? Plan ahead. Hopefully, you won't have to use the plan, but you and your family will be happy you have it if you need long-term care services.

Long-term care policies are designed to spring into action when a person can no longer perform two or three specific activities of daily living—bathing, dressing, eating, transferring, toileting, and continence. Usually there is also coverage for certain cognitive impairments without the need to meet the two to three "activities of daily living" criteria. Alzheimer's disease or dementia will normally qualify a person to be eligible to receive the benefits from a long-term care policy.

Many people think Medicare pays for these long-term care services, but Medicare pays for only a very small amount of long-term care services. Medicare pays for "skilled care" while long-term care policies are designed to help defray the costs of "custodial care." Skilled care requires a medical professional, but custodial care includes the activities of daily living mentioned above. Custodial care is what most people in these situations need.

Medicaid (welfare) does have provisions for long-term care services, but you have to meet poverty line requirements to be eligible. You cannot have over a certain amount of assets. Some people try to spend down or transfer assets into another person's name but the government can look back up to five years and penalize those who have tried to play this game. Don't play games. Just plan ahead and get the protection.

Easy as 1 2 3

Long-term care policies are designed to spring into action when a person can no longer perform two or three specific activities of daily living— bathing, dressing, eating, transferring, toileting, and continence.

Please meet with a professional in this industry to review options, terms, and conditions. Compare quotes, coverage, companies, and agents/representatives. This is an important product essential to protecting one's assets. The plan also gives people choices on services/facilities and provides control over their situation to a certain extent.

Homeowners Insurance

You live and sleep with this P.A.L.! I guess you should know this one pretty well, huh? Your biggest asset likely depends on this P.A.L.

for protection. Your home is your castle, and you want to make sure it has the proper coverage to repair or replace it if trouble strikes. Remember, a flood is not covered by your homeowners policy though. You can purchase a separate flood policy for that type of protection. There are also certain exclusions and limitations of coverage so meet with your agent or insurance professional to review the coverage you have to make sure it meets your needs.

Remember, a flood is not covered by your homeowners policy.

Let's look at a few areas of coverage you may want to review in your own policy:

- **Personal articles policy**—This policy provides additional coverage for expensive items and items that have special limits on them. Some common items in this category include jewelry, furs, computers, firearms, goldware/silverware, and antiques.

- **Sewer/drain backup**—Homeowners policies exclude this coverage, but you can buy it back. I highly recommend any homeowner add this coverage. If you have this type of problem, you'll wish you had the coverage. The endorsement provides protection for raw sewage backing up into the home. See your insurance provider for further details.

- **Business in the home**—Your homeowners policy is designed to protect "personal" liability and "personal" property. Some policies allow you to add certain business riders to the homeowners policy to provide protection for the business.

- **Who Is Insured?** — I used to run across this problem from time to time when I was handling claims. George and Mary get engaged. Mary moves in with George. They are living together. Someone breaks into the home or apartment and steals various items. George has a homeowners or renters policy to cover the property. Seems okay, right? Well, if Mary isn't added to the policy, her property likely won't be covered. They are not married or related and she is not a minor so she won't fit the definition of an insured by most insurance companies. So, fiancés and significant others who are living together, make sure this base is covered. You can just add the person onto the policy as a "named insured" to solve this problem. There is normally no additional cost to do this.

Liability Insurance

This P.A.L. tags along with some of your other P.A.L.s. Liability protection is built into some other policies (such as auto, home, and boat policies), but you can purchase additional protection to cover you in those extraordinary cases where your basic liability limits are not enough. This policy is called an umbrella policy because it provides an umbrella of additional protection over many different risk exposures. The policies normally start at $1 million of additional protection. What does this mean to you? If you have a substantial claim that exceeds your basic liability limits, the umbrella policy will kick in to provide an additional $1 million (or more) to protect you.

People think they will never experience a liability situation, but that's what everyone thinks and it does happen to people. Do you think you're immune to the trials of life? Stuff happens to people every day. That's why insurance companies are in business. As you know, part of my experience as a financial and insurance professional includes several years working as a claim representative for a major insurance company. I've seen some interesting things and handled some interesting claims. I've handled dog bite claims and death claims. Here are some situations I've seen turn into claims:

Easy as 1 2 3

People think they will never experience a liability situation, but that's what everyone thinks and it does happen to some people. Do you think you're immune to the trials of life? Stuff happens to people every day.

- A house burned down because a child was playing with matches.

- A dog nipped a mail carrier.

- A dog bit a child on the face.

- A child drowned in a pool.

- A person falling and getting injured on the premises of a business or a church.

- The operator of a boat ran over a jet ski and its rider because they didn't see him.

- A driver hit a pedestrian, which put the pedestrian in a coma, because he didn't see the pedestrian crossing the street on a rainy night.

All of these situations actually occurred and resulted in claims. These instances are a very small fraction of the many things that can hap-

pen in day-to-day life. Be smart. Protect yourself and your family. Protect
your assets.

Business Insurance

Your business is your baby. You have
toiled to build it up. Why risk losing
your business over one simple mistake
or misunderstanding?

Your business
coverage can
and should be
tailored to your
particular needs.

If you took the time to start and build your business, why not
take the time to protect it? There are a wide range of occupations
and a wide range of business insurance coverages. Each business is
different and should be covered appropriately. Tailor your coverage
to your business and your needs.

A flower shop needs coverage for refrigeration equipment while
an attorney's office will find malpractice insurance more appropriate.
Some businesses need to add a "peak season" endorsement because
most of their business is conducted during certain peak times. For
example, November and December are huge revenue-generating
months for many retailers. If there were a fire during that time that
caused a disruption of service, a store could lose the majority of its
income for the year.

Certain occupations need specialized coverage in addition to reg-
ular business liability coverage. For example, "errors and omissions"
coverage gives protection to certain professionals for errors that may
have been made and/or omissions that occurred that adversely affected a client. There are many other professional liability policies. If
you deliver a service, research whether you need this coverage.

A company with employees may need "employee dishonesty"

coverage to provide protection just in case employees get sticky fingers and steal from the company.

Also, if you're a business owner with employees, you need Worker's Compensation insurance. This policy gives protection to employees who are injured on the job while doing tasks that are within their scope of employment.

There are so many different ways for a business policy to come into play. I remember an interesting claim filed against a painting contractor. The painter painted the exterior of a building with his sprayer. No big deal, right? Job done. Give him the check, and he's on to the next job. Well, it was windy that day and his paint ended up on a parking lot full of people's cars. That was a big deal. Well, my company ended up paying for a car lot full of paint jobs.

Easy as 1 2 3

Equipment floaters are a common need for contractors (and any business or company that takes their business property off premises).

Equipment floaters are a common need for contractors (and any business or company that takes their business property off premises). Business policies typically only cover business property on the premises and up to one hundred feet away from the insured location. Well, many contractors take their tools off the premises to complete their work. They have to. But if something happens to the tools, there is a major problem. Get the proper coverage.

I remember receiving a homeowners claim one day for some tools that were damaged while in the homeowner's truck. The truck caught on fire outside his house. The homeowners policy covers fire and it covers the homeowner's personal tools. But, when I got more details, the situation turned grim. The tools were "business tools." The truck was his Mac Tools truck. There were $10,000 worth of tools in the truck. He needed a business policy on those tools. The homeowners policy didn't cover it.

Get the proper coverage for your business. You'll be glad you did. Hey, it's not costly and it's a write off. You can lower your taxable income!

Life insurance can help you preserve your assets so you can leave a legacy to your family.

Life Insurance

This P.A.L. can help you preserve your assets so you can leave a legacy to your family. Your assets will stay in the family and allow your family options. Your family will be able to continue their standard of living because your P.A.L. will be there for them. Your children will be able to enjoy a life without various hardships and avoid many obstacles because your P.A.L. will provide for their every need. This P.A.L. will make the difference between the family continuing on or slamming into financial woes.

Make sure your beneficiaries are listed as you wish. These are the people who will receive the proceeds of the life insurance policy. Always list a primary beneficiary(ies) AND a contingent/successor beneficiary(ies). The contingent (successor) beneficiary(ies) is the person who will receive the benefit if the primary beneficiary isn't around (may have died or can't be found). Check your beneficiaries every year (or after a major event—marriage, divorce, birth of a child, someone's death, etc.). The beneficiaries supersede all other documents and all other people. Your will can't change it. Make sure the policy names the people you want to receive the proceeds.

I had a client who passed away not too long ago and he forgot to change the beneficiaries on one of his life insurance policies. The life policy he had with my office had the correct beneficiary on it—his wife. The other policy was with another company. He never changed the beneficiary, and it named the wrong person—you got it, his ex-wife. That money went to his ex-wife not his current wife. That didn't go over too well.

Life insurance is the least expensive way to establish a legacy. You pay pennies on the dollar for a substantial amount of coverage. When you pass, the proceeds will be left to your named beneficiaries. Where can you get a better return—you pay $20 or $30 a month for a $100,000 benefit? Your age and health are major factors of course.

Easy as 1 2 3

The proper life insurance coverage will enable your family to maintain their standard of living because your P.A.L. will be there for them.

Over the years I've heard countless objections to the idea of life insurance. I'd like to dispel some of the more common objections right here.

- **"I have it at work..."** Work coverage is rarely enough and you usually can't take it with you when you leave. It's best to lock in a rate with a "personal" plan so the plan follows you and the coverage is always in force.

- **"I'm young and don't have any dependents or a mortgage..."** It's best to lock in coverage while you can because you can't guarantee you'll be in good health later. The older you get, the more it costs. Think forward and obtain some coverage now (at your current age and health) in anticipation of your future responsibilities (spouse, children, and home).

- **"I'm too old…"** Be responsible and at least purchase a small plan. If you're that old, you should know better than to leave people financially strapped. I'm sure you've seen it happen plenty of times in your lifetime.

- **"It costs too much…"** Most plans cost less than a night out to dinner. Consider sacrificing something else that adds no value to you, your family, or your legacy if you have to (like cable, lotto, shopping, jewelry, cars, alcohol, cigarettes, or hanging out). I know of situations where people had a preferred rate but let a policy lapse. The next thing you know the person is uninsurable, yet they have many people relying on them (spouse and children). Was it better to let the life policy lapse or let go of the cable (or some other unimportant bill)? Which expense serves as a benefit that may touch generations to come?

- **"Let them make it on their own…"** This is plain irresponsible! Do the right thing. The cost is minimal to provide a legacy.

Everyone needs protection. I've processed claims for people of all ages—from very small children to teenagers to young adults to seniors. The reasons vary. It's almost always unexpected, and it is always tragic. Life insurance can't change that, but it can help tremendously in such a difficult situation.

I recommend completing a life insurance review to see how much coverage you need. This review should be based on your numbers, but make sure you include certain categories. Most life insurance professionals will give you a few categories to plug in numbers and come up with your ideal amount of coverage. All coverage should include the following:

- **Final expenses**—This pays for funeral costs, which average $6,000.

- **Income replacement**—This should be 60-80 percent of your current combined income, because if one person is gone, their expenses leave too. If the annual income was $100,000, then $60,000 to $80,000 will be the income for the survivors. Then you need to determine how many years you would like this amount to be provided to your family. Most people choose to have the income continue until the last child is out of school. If there are no children, then people commonly choose to continue the income for five to ten years. For an example, let's say there is a ten-year-old child, and we need $80,000 per year. The total coverage needed for this category would be $960,000 (12 times $80,000).

- **Debt**—This pays off outstanding debt (mortgages, credit cards, car loans, student loans, consolidated loans, and personal loans). Suppose you have a $300,000 mortgage, $5,000 in credit card debt, and $20,000 in car loans, then you would need coverage of $325,000.

- **Education fund**—This can be either a flat amount or the actual cost based on the college that the child may attend. The average public college cost for 2008-2009 is $6,585 a year. Average private college costs for 2008-2009 is a little over $25,000 a year. We'll use the public school figure, so four years at $6,585 a year totals $26,340 for a four-year education at a public school. (College costs obtained from www.collegeboard.com.)

The sum of these categories equals $1,317,340 ($6,000 + $960,000

+ $325,000 + $26,340). It's fine to trim back some areas, but you want to know what you're choosing and the consequences of those choices.

After you ascertain your ideal amount of coverage, you need to answer two more questions:

1. How long do you want the coverage to last?
2. What is your budget?

These are two very important questions. Do you need coverage for a short period of time or do you need permanent coverage? How much money can you afford to spend? Once you've thought through those answers, it's time to consider the type of coverage/policy you want.

There are several types of life insurance policies. They each have different features and costs. Let's do a quick review of the most common ones:

- **Term life**—Term life is the most economical type of life insurance. Term eventually "terminates," which means it lasts only for a certain period of time. Term life insurance will leave you without coverage at some point (age 75, 85, 95). The rate is locked in for a certain period of time—ten years, twenty years, thirty years. But after that term (period of time), the rate will increase drastically often to the point of being cost prohibitive. Term life builds no cash value.

- **Whole life**—Whole life (also called permanent life insurance) costs quite a bit more than term because of its multiple benefits. The policy never expires and the premium never increases. It also builds cash value that can be used by the policy owner and has a guaranteed death benefit. The only way to access the cash value of the policy is through a policy loan. The life insurance company will charge interest on that loan.

- **Universal life** — Universal life is a flexible life insurance policy that costs more than term life but less than whole life. It has a cash value feature and can be manipulated to last indefinitely. The Universal life plan doesn't have a guaranteed death benefit like whole life however. There is normally a guaranteed minimum interest rate that is paid toward the account value. The cash value can be "withdrawn" from the policy by the policy owner instead of a loan-only option like whole life. This money does not have to be returned to the policy but it will affect the longevity of the policy and the account value. There is also a loan option with the UL. A loan can be taken against the cash value in the policy with a corresponding interest rate assessed.

Easy as 1 2 3

Some life insurance is better than none. Get coverage in place even if it's not your ideal policy or your ideal amount.

Some people are passionate about one product and dislike another. Get informed, make a decision, and get a policy. Get protected. Like what you like, but get something in place. Something is better than nothing, even if it's not your ideal policy or your ideal amount.

Don't procrastinate. After you verify the integrity and financial strength of the company you're considering (and the integrity of the representative), move forward. There are two big factors that should keep you from waiting. The first is age. The older you get, the more life insurance costs. I am amazed at the number of people who have told me they thought life insurance costs less the older you get. The older you are, the closer you are to dying. Sorry to be so blunt, but it's true. As you age, the life insurance company is getting closer to paying out a death benefit because your chances of dying increase every year. For that reason a life insurance policy for a sixty-year-old will cost more than a policy for a forty-year-old in the same health condition. That leads me to my second factor. No one can guarantee their health. One week you could be fine, and the next week you could be diagnosed with something that increases your rate or makes you ineligible.

Let me give you an example. I completed a life review with a client one year. She needed $500,000 based on her figures. She wanted to get $250,000 one year and come back for the remaining $250,000 the following year. Of course I discourage that unless this is the only amount that fits the client's budget. She applied and qualified for preferred rates, and her $250,000 policy was issued. The following year she came back for more coverage, but she had a health ailment that bumped her out of preferred status and into an increased rate status. She couldn't afford the rate for the additional policy since her health was not in good order. Fortunately, the preferred rate she had on the initial policy was locked in so she didn't have to worry about it changing during the locked-in term.

Believe it or not, I've had clients come in one week and say they'll be back for the life insurance coverage. The next week I've received a call from a spouse or girlfriend asking if the person got the life insurance policy because the person has died. They never made it back in to get the policy. Spouses, children, and significant others are left financially strapped.

Get coverage now. Lock in your rate. Don't wait. Age, health, and life itself are moving targets. Seize the here and now.

There are other life insurance polices but the ones we've discussed are the most common. Speak with your life insurance professional for more information on which product will best fit your needs.

Your Will

I just wanted to quickly mention this P.A.L. Please make sure you have a will. This document makes things easier on those left behind and explains exactly how you want your property distributed. Your will states your desires and eliminates the guesswork. The document is not expensive, $250 or so based on how simple or complicated you make it, but it will be appreciated by those you leave behind. There's no need to add more stress to an already emotional situation.

Easy as 1, 2, 3

Much of the insurance coverage that people have to buy (because the state or a lending institution requires it) protects others.

Insurance 101

Much of the insurance coverage that people have to buy (because the state or a lending institution requires it) protects others. The state normally requires people carry insurance, such as auto insurance, to protect others. Lending institutions normally require insurance to protect their own interests (their stake in your car and home). Business owners (like contractors) often have to provide a "certificate of insurance" before they are accepted for a job. No certificate of insurance, no job. No job, no money.

People actually buy insurance in reverse order. They make sure the property insurance is in place first. This is mainly due to requirements either by the state or a lending institution. Sometimes potential clients require business owners to show proof of insurance before allowing the business to perform any work for them. People "have to" buy this coverage, but look who it protects—others. What about you, your family, and your business? What kind of protection do *you* have?

Insurance should protect *your* interests, not just the interests of others.

If the state, lending institutions, and potential clients are smart enough to require protection shouldn't you look into making sure you're adequately protected too? Fortunately, auto and home insurance policies provide protection to policyholders for damage to the property and/or liability arising out of owning the property. But who keeps the bank from taking the property when you can't afford it because your income has decreased or has been eliminated? Be sure to look out for your best interests not just the lender's.

Liability coverage is built into business policies too. But what happens if someone steals your equipment or what if your computer crashes? Where is *your* protection?

I consider Insurance 101 the basics of insurance. The basics of insurance should include protecting your interest, not just the interest of others. It's good ol' self-preservation. You want to make sure you obtain coverage that provides the right protection to enable you to keep the possessions you have acquired. Imagine the devastation that could ensue if an income was lost or some other tragedy occurred causing you to lose your stuff. The bank will merely re-sell the home to someone else. Close this gap and make sure you are implementing the principle of Insurance 101—self-preservation.

Obtain plans such as disability income protection, life insurance, health insurance, and long-term care protection, and build your emergency savings to protect you and your family. These plans are asset and income protectors. Their main focus is YOU!

Please obtain coverage outside of work for plans like disability insurance and life insurance. If the plans at work are economical and have a good benefit, it may be fine to keep them too but you shouldn't tie such important plans to your place of employment. As this

Easy as 1 2 3

If you feel you don't have the money for insurance, then ask yourself whether you are wealthy enough to self-insure.

recent economic downturn has reminded us, employment isn't guaranteed. As people lose their job, they lose their benefits. Group insurance normally does not follow you. That's why it's called "group" insurance. It's tied to a group. When you leave the group, you leave the insurance.

Sometimes there is an option to take the plan with you, but the rate often explodes through the roof. It's simpler to have your own personal plan that follows you wherever you go. Most group policies are often insufficient. For example, group life insurance may be one or two times your salary, but most people need far more coverage than that.

I know many people feel that they don't have the money for insurance. If you feel that way, then you have to ask yourself whether you are wealthy enough to self-insure. Every time you decide against choosing a particular P.A.L., you are deciding to self-insure. You are saying, "I am wealthy enough to take care of whatever that P.A.L. would have handled." There are some people just that wealthy, but that's a very small fraction of the population. As a matter of fact, most wealthy people have a lot of P.A.L.s because they know it's much more cost effective and wise to have the P.A.L.s than not to have the P.A.L.s. It's pretty simple math.

I hope you realize and accept the fact that life is a lot easier, safer, and less stressful with your P.A.L.s around. These companions help you maintain stability and grow toward financial success. Take control of the "what ifs." Don't let the "what ifs" take control of you.

Easy as $\dfrac{1}{3}\dfrac{2}{}$

Easy as 1 2 3

Use It, Don't Lose It

I wrote this book to provide you with some basic tips on handling your finances. The language is plain. The points are simple. I didn't want to get too detailed or complicated, because that can make money management seem out of reach and unrealistic. I hope now you know that money management is for everyone. I wanted you to have a basic outline to start you on the right track. Don't get discouraged. Don't give up before you get started. Decide to improve your financial situation, and take baby steps. You really can take control of your finances and your future.

Knowledge alone is not power. When you use the knowledge, it gives you power. I believe I have given you the knowledge. Now,

I hope you implement the knowledge to exercise power over your financial life.

Remember, money management is as easy as 1, 2, 3:

1. Control M.I.M.O.
2. Put your money in the right places.
3. Always keep your P.A.L.s around.

Take care. Happy finances to you!

Easy as 1 2 3

Easy as 1 2 3

Thank You!

First, I would like to give honor and praise to my Lord and Savior Jesus Christ. Without Him I am nothing. I thank Jesus daily for blessing me and allowing me to live because there is nothing I did to deserve it. There is nothing I did to deserve His favor but He granted it. Jesus protected me and watched over me when I was not making the best decisions. He's still doing that. He's such an awesome God.

Thanks to my lovely and beautiful wife, Jeronda Burley. She is beautiful inside and out. She is so supportive of me in everything I do and I am very appreciative of that. She is MPQ—My Precious Queen. Our marriage is a divine connection. Jeronda gives me balance. I respect what she says and I give heavy weight to what she says. She's a woman of God and lives it daily. Her bright insight oftentimes makes me realize I'm not always the sharpest knife in the drawer! This is very important because no one knows it all. I love her dearly for being who she is, for all she does, and for all she means to me.

I definitely have to thank my parents. The Lord blessed me with wonderful parents. I thank the Lord all the time for them. My mom, Ollie Burley, and my dad, Ernest Burley, have shaped my life. They were there every step of the way. They gave accolades and approval when warranted. They also released the rod of correction when it was needed. They provided me a loving home and demonstrated before me countless good character traits—reverence to God, honesty, integrity, positive work ethic, charity, compassion, respect, and discipline. I don't take that for granted because many people don't have that. My parents' values are imprinted in me forever. They are a true blessing to me. The Lord worked through them to make me the man I am today.

My dad passed away on October 17, 2005. That was very hard for me. It still is. He was only sixty-two years old. Dad instilled so many values in me. I saw how he conducted himself as a man and a provider. I saw how he honored God and maintained good relationships with people. I saw how he was prudent with his money. I saw how he was a giver and liked to help people. I saw how he liked to socialize with people. I saw how he liked to share his knowledge with people. I saw how he liked to see young people move ahead and take care of their families. I saw how he respected his parents and his elders. He was a great man. Dad I love you and I miss you as my eyes form tears just by thinking about you and what you meant to me and so many other people.

My mom is such a sweet person. She is a jewel. My mom always gave me encouragement and believed in me. She gave me inspiration. She always told me I could be whatever I wanted to be. She let me dream and gave me words of affirmation. Even now she says I could have been the President of the United States! When she says it, I believe it. While I was growing up I saw my mom dream and pursue her dreams. I saw her spirit of entrepreneurship and vision of bigger things. I get my creativity and "out the box" thinking from her. She is a wonderful woman and a godly woman. My mother is also a people person. People are drawn to her because of her personality, her compassion, and her genuineness. Mom and dad set the example for me to follow. I am a mixture of them and I thank God for that formula—mom, dad, and God.

Finally, my extended family and friends surely deserve mention because they helped shape my life too. Even though I was born in New York and raised in Miami, my family is deeply rooted in the big city of Camilla, Georgia. Never heard of it? Well, it's not really that big. Some have moved out of Camilla but there are still many left there. I thank them for what they mean to me, in Camilla and all across the country. I love them all!

Thanks also to my dear friends. We don't stay in contact as much as we'd like due to "life," but we know we're there for each other. I can't forget my precious little godchildren. They're adorable and I love them dearly.

Easy as 1 2 3

About the Author

Ernest Burley, Jr. is a CERTIFIED FINANCIAL PLANNER™ practitioner and Chartered Financial Consultant® who has over twenty years of experience helping people in the insurance and financial services arena. He also holds the CPCU® designation (Chartered Property Casualty Underwriter) and AIS designation (Associate in Insurance Services). He has a passion for helping people properly manage their money and protect their assets. Ernest delivers presentations and has spoken to churches, client groups, and fellow financial services professionals both locally and across the country. People are drawn to his honesty, knowledge, competence, personality and easy-to-understand message.

His call-in radio talk show, *Financial V.I.T.A.L. Signs*, airs every Sunday from 3-4 p.m. EST on WOL 1450AM (a Radio One station). Ernest also created the V.I.T.A.L. proVISIONS scholarship fund in 2005. He has awarded four scholarships to date.

Ernest is married to his lovely wife of two years, Jeronda. They reside in Maryland just 30 minutes outside of the nation's capitol, Washington D.C. Ernest owns an insurance and financial services firm in the area.

More Info

Go to www.moneymanagementeasyas123.com to order this book. All you have to remember is the title and you have the website address! See, easy as 1, 2, 3. I encourage you to buy/order the book for you AND those you know – family, friends, coworkers, church members, educators… This book will make a positive difference in their lives (and yours) once they start applying the principles.

For information on booking Ernest for various venues, please email financialvitalsigns@yahoo.com. Ernest is available for book signings, seminars, consulting and various speaking engagements.

Join Ernest Burley, Jr. every Sunday from 3-4 p.m. EST during his call-in radio show, Financial V.I.T.A.L. Signs, on WOL 1450AM (a Radio One station). Log in anywhere in the country online at www.wolam.com. Have a question? Want to join the conversation or make a comment? Call in! 1-800-450-7876. We can speak live on the air or off the air. Fresh topics and/or guest experts are featured weekly.

For more information on Ernest Burley, Jr.'s V.I.T.A.L. proVI-SIONS Scholarship Fund please contact them at: financialvital-signs@yahoo.com. The V.I.T.A.L. proVISIONS Scholarship Fund is a 501(c)(3) non-profit corporation so donations are tax deductible. Those who want to help our future leaders attend college, please send donations to:
V.I.T.A.L. proVISIONS,
13621 Annapolis Rd, Bowie, MD 20720.
Make checks payable to V.I.T.A.L. proVISIONS.
Please include your return address so we can send a receipt for your tax-deductible donation.

CPSIA information can be obtained at www.ICGtesting.com
Printed in the USA
BVOW041418190313

315848BV00002B/8/P